Living in
Spain

Written by Su Kent

Photographed by David Hampton

W

FRANKLIN WATTS
LONDON•SYDNEY

This edition 2005

Franklin Watts
96 Leonard Street
London EC2A 4XD

Franklin Watts Australia
Level 17/207 Kent Street
Sydney NSW 2000

Series editor: Ruth Thomson
Series designer: Edward Kinsey
Additional photographs: Spanish Tourist
Office pages 5(b), 8(l), 17(fl), 19(tr), 22(l),
23 (tr, br), 26(c), 27(t), 29(br); Catalonia Tourist
Board frontispiece, 9(c), 12(c), 13(tl), 28(r),
29(tl); Turgalicia 4(l); Carrefour 16(l); Rachel
Hamdi 9(r), 15(tr, br), 19(br); Neil Thomson
4(r), 8(c), 9(l), 10(l), 11(l), 14(c, r), 15(tc), 23(tc);
Edward Kinsey 11(r), 16(c), 17(fl), 18(l),
20(l, cr), 26(l), 28(bl).

With thanks to Sarah Blyth

A CIP catalogue record for this book
is available from the British Library

Dewey Classification 919.4

ISBN 0 7496 6344 8

Printed in Malaysia

DOÑA JIMENA
DE ESPAÑA

SPECIALITIES FROM SPAIN

EXPIRY DATE / LOT.
SEE REVERSE OF PACK

FECHA DE CADUCIDAD / LOTE
VER REVERSO DEL ESTUCHE

PESO NETO • POIDS NET • INHALT •
PESO NETTO • PESO LIQUIDO:
NET WEIGHT
270 g. e-9'5 oz. e
MADE IN SPAIN

Avda. de la
Constitución, s/n
Tel. 95 456 33 21
Fax 95 456 47 43
41001 SEVILLA
C.I.F. Q-4100146-B

ACCESO AL TESORO,
SACRISTIA Y GIRALDA

TICKET N°
3 ENTRA
ADULTOS
2400
14 42
/27/200

Contents

This is Spain

Spain is in south-west Europe. It shares a peninsula with Portugal. The Pyrenees mountains form a natural border with France. The north-west coast faces the Atlantic Ocean. The south and east coasts face the Mediterranean Sea. The southern tip of Spain is only 12 kilometres from the North African coast.

△Sierra Nevada
These mountains, stretching across the south, include mainland Spain's highest peak, Mulhacén (3482 metres).

△The north-west coast
Spain's coastline is more than 8,000km long. The Atlantic coast is wilder and more tidal than the Mediterranean coasts.

▷The plains
A hot, dry plateau (*meseta*) covers most of central Spain. Wheat and maize are the main crops grown here.

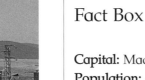

Fact Box

Capital: Madrid
Population: 40 million
National or official languages: Castilian Spanish, Basque, Galician, Catalan
Highest mountain: Mt Teide, Tenerife (3718m)
Biggest cities: Barcelona, Valencia, Seville, Alicante
Longest river: Tagus (1007km)
Main religion: Roman Catholicism
Currency: Euro

Atlantic Ocean

Bay of Biscay

FRANCE

Bilbao •
BASQUE REGION

Pyrenees

R. Douro

PORTUGAL

Guadarrama Mtns

R. Tagus

R. Ebro

CATALUNYA

• Barcelona

• Madrid

Merida •

• Cordoba

• Valencia

• Alicante

Seville •

ANDALUCIA

Granada •

Sierra Nevada

Mt. Mulhacén ▲

Almeria •

Menorca

Majorca

Ibiza

Formentera

Mediterranean Sea

▷**Fishing**
Spain has the largest fishing fleet in Europe.

CANARY ISLANDS

La Palma

Lanzarote

Fuerteventura

Tenerife

▲Mt. Teide

Gomera

Hierro

Gran Canaria

▷**Volcanic islands**
The Canary Islands were thrown up by volcanoes in the Atlantic Ocean, off the west coast of Africa.

Spanish islands

The islands of Majorca, Menorca, Ibiza and Formentera in the Mediterranean Sea are also part of Spain – so too are the seven Canary Islands.

Madrid – the capital

In 1561, the Spanish king, Philip II, moved his court to Madrid, so that the capital was in the centre of the country. It is more than 650 metres above sea level and is the only European capital city without a river that big boats can use. One in ten Spaniards now live here.

A ticket and brochures about some famous sights in Madrid

△ *Grand Via*
This wide avenue cuts through Madrid. It is the commercial heart of the city, lined with banks, shops, offices and cinemas.

◁ **Royal Palace**
The Royal Palace, the Escorial, completed in 1764, has more rooms than any other European palace. It is used for state events by the present king, Juan Carlos I.

6

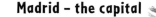

△ **The Prado Museum** *(Museo del Prado)*
The Prado houses Spain's oldest, finest art
collection. It includes paintings by many
famous Spanish artists, such as Velázquez,
Goya and Murillo.

A thriving modern city

Madrid is the centre of government,
industry and banking. The major
industries are textiles, food and metal-
working. The city also has several
museums of art, an opera house, a zoo,
a theme park and a bullring with seats
for over 20,000 people.

▽▷**The** *Retiro*
People come to
this large park
to walk, jog,
cycle, roller-
blade, watch
puppet shows
go boating –
or just to meet
their friends.

Famous sights

The Romans invaded Spain in 200BC. They called it *Hispania*, from which Spain takes its name. Ruins of Roman roads, ports and viaducts can still be seen. North African Moors, who were Muslims, invaded Spain in AD711. They built many mosques and palaces.

▷Alhambra

This Moorish fortified palace in Granada is famous for its great beauty. It is surrounded by red-brick walls that probably gave the palace its name – Alhambra means 'red' in Arabic.

▽Roman theatre

The Roman theatre in Merida was built in 15BC. It can hold 6,000 people. It is still used for drama festivals.

◁Cordoba *Mezquita*

This mosque (*mezquita*) was built by the Moors. Later, Christian kings added two chapels and built a cathedral within the heart of the mosque.

Entrance tickets

Other places of interest

From the 15th century, Christians ruled the whole of Spain again and built many forts, cathedrals and palaces. Some castles, monasteries and palaces have now been converted into grand hotels, called *paradors*.

△Castles

Spain has more than 2,000 castles. Those near the south coast were built against Moorish attack. Others were built as homes for wealthy nobles.

▷*Sagrada Familia*

Gaudí was Spain's most famous architect in the 20th century. His buildings include the *Sagrada Familia* church in Barcelona. This is still being constructed.

▽A film set

The hot desert around Almeria, with its strange rock formations and dried-up riverbeds, is a popular film location.

Life in cities

Just over three-quarters of Spanish people live in towns and cities. With the exception of Madrid, all the main cities are found on the coast. In the centre of every city there is a main square (*Plaza Mayor*), which people use as an everyday meeting place.

△*Plaza Mayor*
The main squares are lined with bars and restaurants. A weekly market takes place in many of them. They may also be used for bullfights, pageants and processions.

△**Seville Cathedral**
Grand churches, like this, were built after Spain discovered the Americas in the 15th century and brought back gold and riches.

▷ **Life outdoors**
On summer evenings, people gather in the town centre to meet friends, stroll about and relax.

City development

In the past 40 years, most towns and cities have grown rapidly, as people have moved from the country to find jobs. Cities are ringed with modern blocks of flats and shopping centres.

△▷Housing

In cities, most people live in flats, often above shops. Some have balconies with flowers.

▽Fountains

The large, splashing fountains in many squares help cool the air on hot summer days.

△City tourism

Every town has a tourist office. This provides maps and guides for visitors.

Life on the coast

The sunny, sandy Mediterranean coasts (the *costas*) and the Balearic and Canary islands attract millions of holidaymakers from all over Europe. Amazingly, there are more visitors to Spain every year than its entire population. Tourism provides all sorts of work for the Spanish.

△Beach holidays
High-rise hotels and flats line the beaches. More and more are built each year.

▷Coastal holidays
Spaniards from inland head for the coast in August when the weather gets very hot.

△Food and drink
Some bars sell English and German food and drink for tourists.

▽Seasonal jobs
Hotels, restaurants, bars and discos provide seasonal work for one in ten Spaniards.

▷Fresh fish
Fishermen provide fresh daily seafood catches for restaurants and hotels.

▽Pottery shop
Spain is famous for its ceramics. Craftspeople make decorated tiles, pots, plates and plant holders. Every region has its own style and designs.

△Aquapark
Some people work in leisure centres, like this one with water slides and swimming pools. They have been built in many holiday resorts.

Tourist industries
Many small industries produce tourist souvenirs. These include hand-made pottery, leather bags and belts, jewellery, lace, textiles and baskets. These industries provide work for local people. Many of them are family-run.

Life in the country

Country life has changed dramatically over the past forty years as Spain has become more industrialised and tourism has grown rapidly. Today, one in ten Spaniards still work the land, although many thousands of people have left the countryside to find work in cities or on the coast.

△**Village streets**
In hill villages, old houses line steep, narrow, cobbled streets.

△**Village people**
There are now more old people than young people in many villages. Small villages are often very isolated from one another.

◁**Changing villages**
New, detached houses have been built on the edge of villages within reach of large cities – either for commuters or as second homes. Old farms have been left to rack and ruin.

△Farming under plastic
Around Almeria, farmers grow vegetables and fruit in vast polythene greenhouses. The crops often grow in a nutrient solution, instead of soil.

△Sunflowers
Sunflowers are grown for their seeds. These are pressed to make cooking oil.

△▷Olives
There are vast olive groves in Andalucia. Spain produces more olive oil than anywhere else in the world.

Olives   *Olive oil*

Farming
In the hot, dry south, farmers grow oranges, olives, grapes, avocados and other fruit. In the cooler north, they grow cereal crops, herd cattle and sheep and keep pigs.

▷Goats
Goats are bred for their milk, which is made into cheese (*queso*).

Shopping

In recent years, many supermarkets and hypermarkets have been built on the edge of towns. These sell lots of convenience foods for busy families. However, many people still shop for food at small grocery stores, speciality food shops and daily (or weekly) markets near their homes.

△**A covered market**
Most districts in cities have their own covered market (*mercado del barrio*). These sell fresh fruit, vegetables, meat, fish, bread and cheese.

△**A hypermarket**
Hypermarkets, furniture stores and clothing outlets are part of huge, new out-of-town retail parks.

◁*El Corte Inglés*
There is a branch of the department store, *El Corte Inglés,* in every big city.

Butcher's shop *(Carnicero)*

Fishmonger *(Pescadería)*

Fishmonger *(Pescadería)*

Bakery *(Panadero)*

△**Specialist shops**
People buy fresh food from specialist shops.

▷**Spanish produce**
These are some typical Spanish foods. They are exported around the world.

Almond cake

Smoked paprika

White tuna

Wine

Chorizo (Spicy sausage)

Pimentos

Sardines

On the move

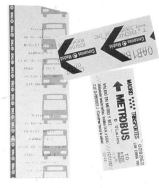

Transport tickets

Only four out of ten Spanish households own a car – far fewer than in other European countries. Public transport in towns and cities is efficient and cheap. Madrid, Barcelona, Valencia and Bilbao have an underground railway *(metro)*.

△▽ Buses

Fares and tickets are the same for both buses and the *metro*. Some new buses in Madrid run on gas, which is better for the environment.

▷ The metro

Madrid's *metro* is the third largest in the world. It has 202 stations and 11 lines that criss-cross the city.

▷ Number plates

Until 2000, the first letters of a number plate showed where a car was registered. M was for Madrid and B was for Barcelona.

▷Fast trains

A high speed AVE train connects Madrid with Seville. It travels up to 300km/h. The 417 km journey takes only two and a half hours.

△Commuter trains

Some trains have two decks to cope with the large number of commuters, who travel into the city for work every day.

▷Motorways

Drivers pay to use some of the motorways *(autopistas)*.

▽Donkeys

In hilly areas, people still use donkeys to carry their crops home from the fields.

Trains and roads

Railways and motorways spread out from Madrid connecting with other large cities. A new motorway runs along the south coast, easing heavy tourist traffic. In remote areas with little traffic, roads are poorly kept.

Family life

Most Spanish families are close knit. They eat many meals together and, at weekends, visit grandparents or go for a stroll (*paseo*). In summer, families spend much of their time outside – having meals in cafés or restaurants with friends and relatives or playing sports.

◁▽Breakfast *(desayuno)*
Breakfast is usually a bowl of cereal, pastries and a chocolate milk drink.

▽Evening meal
Families eat their evening meal together, often around 9pm. Children go to bed after 10pm.

Pastries

Coffee

Hot chocolate mixed with cereal

Toast and honey

◁**Homework**
Children have an hour of homework every night to prepare for frequent tests.

TV guide

◁△**TV viewing**
Popular programmes include Spanish sitcoms and cartoons from America and Japan. Children like *Megatrix* – a mixture of cartoons, activities and games.

Football cards

◁▷**Time to play**
Many boys collect football cards and play football in their nearest playground.

Time to eat

The Spanish use a great deal of olive oil, tomatoes, garlic, onions and peppers in their cooking. Beef, pork, lamb and seafood are eaten everywhere. Some meat dishes are made with fruit and almonds. This type of cooking was introduced to Spain by the Moors.

△Lunch
People eat their biggest meal of the day at lunch time (*comida*). Many restaurants serve lunch from 2pm.

▷Cafés
Many people have a mid-morning snack (*almorzar*). They often eat doughnut strips (*churros*) with a hot drink or juice.

△Menu of the day
By law, as part of their menu, restaurants have to offer a cheap, set price meal. It includes two courses, dessert, bread and a drink.

▽▷ *Tapas*
Tapas bars offer a huge variety of freshly cooked snacks, which people eat after work or between meals.

CASA PLACIDO
BAR
TAPAS

LA GITANA

VINICOLA HIDALGO Y CIA. S.A.
2ª CENTENARIO 1792-1992

Olive oil

Bread (pan)

Salad (ensalada)

Meatballs (albondigas)

△ *Gazpacho*
This cold tomato soup is a refreshing summer dish.

▽ *Paella*
Paella is a rice dish cooked with pork, chicken, fish and shellfish. It is cooked in a shallow pan.

Squid (calamares)

Potatoes with a chilli sauce *(patates bravas)*

Spanish omelette *(tortilla)*

Spicy sausage (chorizo)

School time

Children have to go to school from the age of six until 16. Most go to free state schools. Some go to private, fee-paying ones. Many private schools are run by the Church, where pupils are taught by nuns and priests. All schools follow a national curriculum.

△Going to school
Most children go to a school near their home or to one near where their parents work.

▷Lessons
There are up to 25 pupils in a class. They learn reading, writing, maths, art and science. They begin English lessons at the age of seven.

△School hours
Children go to school from Monday to Friday. Primary schools start at 9:30am and end at 4:30pm. There is a two-hour break for lunch.

▽School bags

Every day, pupils bring the books they need for class in bags with wheels.

△Extra activities

After school, some children learn another language. Others practise Spanish dancing or judo. Many play football. In summer, swimming in outdoor pools is popular.

▽Timetable

Private schools start earlier and finish later than state schools and have an hour for lunch.

Secondary schools

Pupils go to a secondary school at the age of 13. Some leave at 16 and take courses to learn a trade. Others stay on to study for the *bachillerato*, which they have to pass if they want to go to university.

Having fun

The Spanish like to spend time outdoors. In colder months, many of them ski, play ball games or take daily strolls around town. In hot weather, they go swimming in local pools or at the beach. Some people go sailing or windsurfing.

△**A lottery kiosk**
The lottery is very popular. People buy tickets from kiosks run by blind people. The income helps pay for aids for the blind.

△**Rollerskating**
In cities, young people rollerskate in the parks. They also play volleyball, basketball and football.

◁**Skiing**
People ski during winter weekends at ski resorts in the Sierra Nevada, the Pyrenees or the Guadarrama mountains.

▽ **Bullfighting**

Bullfights take place in the summer months. Skilled bullfighters *(matadors)* twist and turn to avoid the charge of fierce bulls.

◁ *Pelota*

In the Basque region, players take turns to hit a hard rubber ball against a wall in a fast game called *pelota*.

Football badges for Real Madrid and F.C. Barcelona

Sports

The Spanish enjoy watching sports. Football is a national passion. Their teams are very successful – Real Madrid has won the European Champions League nine times. Bullfighting and *pelota* are sports that both began in Spain.

Celebrations

There are religious and folk festivals *(fiestas)* throughout the year in Spain. Sometimes, people dress up in the traditional costume of their region. They parade through the streets, dance or perform feats of physical strength and daring.

▽**A human pyramid**
In the Catalunya region, village teams compete to create the highest human pyramid *(casteller)*. When the lightest person reaches the top, he raises his arm in triumph.

▽**Giants**
In Barcelona, people parade giant figures through the streets. The figures dance stiffly to music in the main square.

◁**Flower festival**
In June, many towns hold competitions, where people create carpets of flowers in the street.

◁▷**The Seville Fair (*Feria*)**
During the week-long *feria* in Seville, men wear fitted black suits and women wear bright, layered *flamenco* dresses. They parade in carriages or on horseback and sing and dance.

Going further

Spanish products

Look around a supermarket for foods that have come from Spain. Spanish fruits will usually have a label with *España* on them. Can you find any oils and vinegars produced in Spain? What else can you find?

Design a poster

Make a poster to advertise a flamenco festival. Draw a colourful picture of women with flouncy dresses, head-dresses and clicking castanets. Add a headline and details about the time and place of the event.

Create a carpet

Use the flower carpet competition as inspiration to make one of your own. Glue colourful paper scraps on to a piece of card. You could either make a pattern or choose a typical Spanish image.

Websites

www.yahooligans.com/around_the_world/countries/spain
www.tourspain.es
www.enchantedlearning.com/themes/spanish.shtml
Spain.index.htm
www.cyberspain.com

Glossary

Border The boundary which separates one country from another.

Commuter Someone who travels some distance from home to work each day.

Currency The money used in a country.

Export To send goods or produce from one country to sell in another.

Fertile Fertile land is good for growing crops.

Hypermarket A gigantic superstore that sells a wide range of goods including food, clothes and electrical goods.

Industry The making of goods, from raw materials, for example, making cloth from wool, cotton or nylon, usually in a factory.

Monastery A place where a community of monks live.

Mosque A Muslim place of worship.

Nutrient A chemical substance that helps plants to grow healthily.

Pageant An outdoor entertainment where people dress up in costume and act out scenes from history.

Peninsula Land surrounded by water on three sides and joined on one side to a larger land mass.

Plain A large area of open flat land.

Plateau A flat highland.

Population The number of people who live in one particular place, such as a town or country.

Seasonal Describes something that is affected by or changes with the seasons.

Suburb The outer area of a town or city where many people live.

Viaduct A long, arched bridge that takes a road over a wide valley or river.

Volcano A cone-shaped mountain lying over an underground chamber of molten rock. Sometimes pressure from hot gases causes a volcano to erupt.

Index

Page numbers in *italics* refer to entries in the fact box, on the map or in the glossary.